The

DEDICATION

    This book is dedicated to my heavenly Father for who he is in my life. Blessed Holy Spirit, you are truly amazing and reverence by me.

The Prophet's Instructions

TABLE OF CONTENTS

THE MANTLE OF THE PROPHET

In this chapter, I will explain what it means to serve a Prophet and how to receive their mantles. A Prophet's mantle was a special garment that was worn during their time in their office. We see how Elijah wore the mantle that he released to his successor Elisha (1 King 19:18).

Our motives should not be just the mantle, but to serve the Prophet without the intention of getting his mantle and go about our business. It is extremely important to respect and honor the Prophet the intention of

3

The Prophet's Instructions

getting his mantle and go about our business. It is extremely important to respect and honor the Prophet you serve.

Most people who serve Prophets become too familiar with the Prophets, and their anointing. Familiarity breeds contempt and if you are not careful, you can serve a Prophet for years but never receive his or her mantle (Mark 6:1-6). We must have the spirit of humility in our daily walk with the Prophet. As we read the scriptures, we do not see anywhere in the bible where Joshua and Caleb badmouthed

The Prophet's Instructions

Moses, their leader. What is happening with this generation is the fact we want mantles without submission. You are not reading this book by accident, but by divine instructions from the Holy Spirit. Moses had an anger issue that caused him to miss the promise land (Exodus 32:19).

Our bible declares, touch not my anointed and do my Prophets no harm (1Chronicles 16:22). The anointing you respect, God will allow you to walk in it and even greater. Elisha served Elijah with persistence, love, respect, honor, patience, gratitude and so forth. We have the laws of God and the principles of God. One of God's principles is, you cannot mistreat His Prophets.

God is jealous and protective over His Prophets. I remember the showdown with Elijah and the false Prophets of Baal. Elohim will always back up His anointed ones, the Prophets (1 Kings 18: 20-40). I have heard people tell me, Prophets these days do not carry the same anointing as the old testaments Prophets. The answer to this question is no because God is the same yesterday, today and forever more. Our God does not

The Prophet's Instructions

change nor His promises for anyone. They referred to Elisha as the one who poured water on the hands of Elijah (2 Kings 3:11).

Many of us will not receive the Prophet's mantle because we do not serve wholeheartedly. I truly believe the majority of us would not have received Elijah's mantle. Are you willing to go to the assignment which God assigns the Prophet to go? Elisha forsook everything to follow Elijah without him getting paid. When it is God who called you to walk with a Prophet, He will take care of you and your family. I want to say to you, do not allow hardship, lack of honor and disobedience to disconnect you from your assigned Prophet. Again, most people who serve Prophets are not loyal nor committed.

They want to see their success and not their failure. When God shows you something about the Prophet you serve, your first reaction should be, I am standing in prayer for him or her without publicize their weaknesses. We want mantles without knowing what we signed up for. The Prophet's mantle is costly and they continue to pay a heavy price for it. You need to celebrate your Prophet daily.

Learn how to sow in their lives as the pour their experiences, anointing, wisdom and the spirit of excellence. The bible lets us know in Matthew ten verse forty one, if we receive a Prophet in the name of a prophet, we shall have a prophet's reward. The reward is whatever is in the possession of the Prophet becomes yours.

How do we receive the reward of a Prophet? We must to see them how God sees them and treat them the way He treats them. When you do

The Prophet's Instructions

not receive a Prophet properly, God will close their mouth and you will not be able to receive anything from them. When you hear people talking bad about God's Prophet, if you were there, run as fast as you can. People of God, stop mocking the Prophets. God will remove them from your midst and bless someone else with them.

The shunamite woman said, I perceive he is a holy man of God (2 Kings 2:3). Her perception granted her what money could not have given her. My beloved, just because everybody else do not appreciate

The Prophet's Instructions

their set Prophets, make sure it is not you. I Pastor an awesome church in North Miami Beach Florida where the sons and daughters who value me and the anointing upon my life. They walk in the prophetic without limitation. I attract what I value and what I value will be imparted to me. The sons of the Prophets knew God was about to take Elijah to heaven but never served him (2 Kings 2:3).

Some people will never serve you even though the anointing over your life can raise the dead and heal the sick. Elisha was not concerned about just knowing when God was

The Prophet's Instructions

going to take Elijah to heaven but he wanted the mantle of his predecessor (2 Kings 2:9). You will find people, all they know is God using you, but never come close to be a partaker of what He is doing in your life.

When I turned thirty four, a friend of mine who is a millionaire took me out for my birthday. As I sat across from him, he said to me Stanley, why are you not asking me how I became a millionaire. The only thing that was in my mind was, he is going to bless me financially today.

What do we do when we get around the Prophets? We do not ask

The Prophet's Instructions

question and all we want is a word from the Prophet. We must have a mindset to pick up their brain and receive something that will change our destiny forever. As God sends a Prophet to mentor you, do not be common with them even if they are your family members.

What the millionaire was saying to me nonverbally was, you just want me to bless you just for your birthday while I can deposit a financial mantle that will be on you for the rest of your life. Elisha asked for the double of Elijah's spirit (2 Kings 2:9). Some ask for the double

The Prophet's Instructions

portion of the anointing while Elisha wanted double portion of Elijah's spirit (2 Kings 2:9). When asked for the double portion of his spirit, he said to himself, I want the prophetic, the miracles he walked in and the signs of wonders. Elijah carried an anointing of two Kings and a Prophet.

That anointing was heavy on Elijah therefore Elisha saw all the miracles and he was not going to let go unto he received the mantle. Let me release this revelation to you as I close this chapter. The reason why Gehazi did not receive the mantle

The Prophet's Instructions

was because, he was greedy, disobedient, and negligent and did not following proper instructions from his master. Learn how to follow the Prophet's instructions and your life will be bless (2 Kings 5:20-27).

My prayer for you: Dear Lord, teach me how to be obedient to your servant as he or she take me under their wings. I will not allow my emotions to make me miss what you have for me through him or her. I pray you walk in the spirit of humility and honor as you serving the Prophet.

The Prophet's Instructions

THE AUTHORITY OF THE PROPHET

God gives Prophets authority in the earth realm as well as in the spiritual realm. When Elijah declared no rain for three years and half, the heavens agreed with his request (1 Kings 17:1). A Prophet is a representative of God on the earth. People who do not understand a Prophet's grace, will never be okay with their office of the Prophet.

Elijah said, at my word it will not rain 1 Kings 17:1). God loves when His Prophets walk in boldness

The Prophet's Instructions

and faith. Elijah had so much faith to
the point he told the shunamite
woman, next year by this time you
shall conceive a son (2 Kings 4:1-17).
Elohim did not tell him to declare it
over the woman but he knew the kind
of God he served.

When we do not speak, God
cannot make anything come to pass.
Some Prophets have authority over
governments, states, cities and
countries. The bible says, from Dan
to Beersheba they knew Samuel was
established as a Prophet (1 Samuel
3:19-20). It was the whole Israel that
God gave Samuel authority over.

The Prophet's Instructions

When you have authority over something, it means what you say go. Prophet Daniel had authority in the Babylonians government (Daniel 1:6).

Prophets whom God gives authority in certain realms, can change the financial situations, change the weather, stop crimes and allow the people to walk in freedom. The Lord spoke to Moses and told him, I will make you a God to Pharaoh (Exodus 7:1). Which means he had authority over Egypt and the King. Moses took the children of Israel from bondage to freedom

The Prophet's Instructions

(Exodus 14). Their authority is so strong, they can speak on your behalf and what they say will be in your favor. When Elisha spoke to the King on behalf on the shunamite woman, he restored everything back to her (2 Kings 8:1-6).

Your Prophet has the ability to make a request for you, it will surely happen. When I encounter some individual, the first question I asked them is, are you connected to a Prophet? A Prophet carries the anointing of prosperity, healing, and deliverance. When the shunamite son died, she went to the Prophet because

The Prophet's Instructions

it was the Prophet who caused her to conceive a child even in her old age (2 Kings 4:27). I myself is connected to Prophets. At times, you need to hear what the Lord is saying concerning your life. I remember the story of the widow who said to the Prophet the creditors are coming to get my sons because of what my husband owed them.

He asked her what you have in your house. She said a little of oil and we will eat and die. He asked her bake me the first cake (1 King 17:13). To some of us, we would rather die than bake the Prophet the cake. She

The Prophet's Instructions

did not know the Prophet carried an anointing that was going to multiply the little she had. You do not go to a Prophet empty handed. You always have to have a seed in your hands to bless. Sa ul would not have been King if it was not for the seed he brought to Samuel. Samuel did not ask for a seed but Saul knew he was going before someone who could hear from God to tell him where the donkey was.

You see, when you honor the Prophet that God places in your life, you will walk and know things you have never known before. When we

The Prophet's Instructions

read Hosea twelve verse thirteen, it says, by a Prophet Israel came out and by a Prophet she was preserved. The Prophet's authority has the ability to take you out of whatever you are in and preserve you from calamity.

Moses had such an anointing upon his life for the children of Israel. God used him mightily to bring them out of their bondage. A Prophet who knows his authority in the natural as well in the spiritual is dangerous. Prophets may not be friendly, but what they carry can bless you and your entire household.

THE PROPHET'S INSTRUCTIONS

Prophets come with instructions in their spirit which they will release through their mouth. When we do not follow the instructions of the Prophets, we will miss big on what God has for us. Prophets come to reveal the mind and the intent of God.

We see how Elijah gave the widow of Zarephath an instruction concerning his meal. Once the widow obeyed his instruction, then, the heavens were open on her behalf. Most of us today would say, how the

The Prophet's Instructions

Prophet can is taking from the poor widow. I want you to understand something concerning God and His prophets. Nothing leaves heaven until there is a sacrifice.

People who cannot follow the instructions the Prophets receive from God for their lives, will never prosper. Instruction is the key when you are in the environment of the Prophets. We remember the story of the wedding in Cana where Mary the mother of our Savior asked Him for a favor (John 2:1-3). Jesus responded to her, woman that does your concern have to do with me? My hour as not

The Prophet's Instructions

yet come (John 2:4). His mother said to them, whatever He says to you, do it. Mary is a type of the Holy Spirit in this verse. His mother was talking to Jesus the Creator who has the power to create anything they needed on that day. Our problem is, we want God to bless us without His instructions.

Jesus is was the Prophet of all Prophets throughout our generation. Prophets are God's representative in the earth realm and God honor their words when they speak over your life. Let me share a revelation with you here. Prophets do not have to

The Prophet's Instructions

hear it from God to declare it over your life. Elisha declared, next year by this time, you shall give birth to a son. The Prophets carry so much authority in the natural and the realm of the spirit.

They carry so much power and revelation to the point God says, I will not do anything unless I reveal my secrets to my servants, the Prophets (Amos 3:7). Prophets have heavenly secrets that most people do not know. Your Prophet is your lifeline. If you do not believe me, ask the children of Israel, they will tell you. Hosea 12:13 declares, by a

The Prophet's Instructions

Prophet Israel came out and by a Prophet she was preserved. As a Christian, you must be connected to a Prophet. When things get tough, the first thing the King would do, they would look for a Prophet to know what direction to go.

I am getting excited as I am releasing these revelations to you. When Jehoshaphat panicked and did not know what to do when he heard the enemies were coming, God raised a Prophet to give the King direction on what to do (1 Kings 22:6). Some people tell me, they do not need a Prophet because God speaks and I

The Prophet's Instructions

always say no problem. They are the first one to call you when they going through something. Make sure you follow the instructions of the Prophet thoroughly.

Joash the King of Israel went to Elisha and cried over his face and said to the Prophet, "O my father, my father, the chariots of Israel and their horsemen (2 Kings 13:14)." Elisha said to him, take a bow and some arrows. So he took it himself a bow and some arrows. Then he said to the King of Israel put your hands on the bow. So he put out his hands on it and Elisha put his hands on the

The Prophet's Instructions

King's hands. The King struck the ground only three times and the Prophet said, you should have struck it five or six times, then you would have struck Syria till you had destroyed it, but now you will strike Syria only three times (2 Kings 13:14-19).

Stop doing what the Prophet told you to do partially. How can we have results when we do not follow the Prophet's instructions? Now, what the Prophet tell you to do, might be contrary to what you normally do or see. Naaman wanted to get healed in a river that was clean, but the

The Prophet's Instructions

Prophet had something else in mind for him (2 Kings 9:15). We cannot tell the Prophets what to do if we really want to be blessed. He left Syria to come to Israel to see the Prophet face to face, but the Prophets in the Old Testament did not really allow people to get in their presence like that.

Elisha told his messenger saying, go and wash yourself in the Jordan seven times and your flesh will be restored to you (2 Kings 5:10). The Jordan River was muddy at that times, but Naaman had no other choice. Even though he was

The Prophet's Instructions

furious, that did not change the
instruction of the Prophet for him.
When he dipped himself in the
Jordan, then he received his healing
through the instruction of God's
mouthpiece. The widow cried to
Elisha saying your servant my
husband is dead and you know he
feared the Lord.

The creditor is coming to take
my two sons to be his slaves. Elisha
said to her, what can I do for you?
Tell me what do you have in your
house (2 Kings 4:1)? The Prophets
need something to work with. The
first question he asked her, what do

The Prophet's Instructions

you have in your house? Can you imagine if she never listened to the instruction of the Prophet? What would have happened? Her sons would be slaves and she would die because of poverty. We should always ask the Prophet, what is the instruction you have for me? A lawyer will ask someone thousands of dollars to get someone out of trouble but we refuse to follow an instruction from the Prophet.

Some people get loans and put their cars and houses on collateral so that our love ones will not stay in jail. How much more should we honor the

The Prophet's Instructions

Prophet who can give us one direction to the point, everything in your life will shift. The Prophet's instruction is vital to your finances, spiritual life, health and so much more. My advice to you is that you follow the instructions they give you. The shunamite woman was connected and remain connected to Elisha afterwards.

One day, there was a famine in Israel and she went to the land of the philistines. After the seven years of the famine, she returned to the land and made an appeal to the King for her house and her land. The King was

The Prophet's Instructions

talking to Gehazi one day and asked
and the good Elisha had done for her
(2 Kings:1-6). As Gehazi was talking
to the King about how Elisha restored
her son back to life, the woman
showed up. She told the King,
everything that Elisha has done for
her.

The King appointed an official
to her and said, restore all that was
hers together with all the revenue of
the field from the day she left the
land until now. The King did not do
it because of her but because she was
connected to Elisha. She was the
same woman who took care of him in

The Prophet's Instructions

his time of needs so when she needed to get to the king, Gehazi only mentioned the name of Elisha and the King restored everything to her. Do you see the benefits you have when you are connected to a Prophet? Everything you need will be at your disposal.

The Prophet's Instructions

RECOVER WHAT WAS LOST

Your Prophet is the one who gives you direction to recover what you have lost. We have our primary doctor when we have a medical issue that we go to. We have a lawyer we contact when we are in trouble. The question I have for you is this, how come you do not have a personal Prophet?

When the shunamite son died, she went to the mountain where he was praying and found him (2 Kings 4:8-7). What if she did not have a relationship with him? In the first place, she could not have children

The Prophet's Instructions

and now the one she had died.
Prophets have direct connection to
heaven and when they speak,
something will take place in your life.
When you are in the midst of a true
Prophet, put a demand on his
anointing.

People get in the company of
the Prophets without expectation.
Expectation will cause the anointing
on their lives to stir up and release
what thus says the Lord. As we read
the story in second Kings Chapter
six, we see how one of the sons of the
Prophets was cutting a tree with an
axe head and it fell in the water. He

The Prophet's Instructions

called the one he was connected to, Elisha the Prophet. What we have to understand is this, metal cannot float on water. Since God's Prophet has the supernatural ability to restore what was lost, he pointed a stick where the axe head fell and found it.

Your prophetic connection restores everything back to you in their original form. Your Prophet carries an anointing that raises the dead things in your life. When Elijah proclaimed the drought in first kings seventeen, God told him that the book dried, go to Zarephath and I command a widow to feed you.

The Prophet's Instructions

When Elijah went, he preserved him and the widow from dying during the famine. Location and obedience is everything when it comes to what God is doing through the Prophet. Elijah was in the right location during the famine. His obedience caused the widow not to die before her time.

God knows who has what you need Prophets in the midst of a famine He will give you directions in which way people should go. Dead things become alive when your Prophet shows up. When the shunamite son died, the Prophet sent his servant to pray so that the boy could come back to life. What the Prophet forgot was the woman was not connected to his servant, but to him.

The very reason why she saddled the donkey and went to him about her dead son was because of the connection they had (2 Kings 4: 8-27). It is vital to connect and remain connected to your Prophet. A woman of God who was not a member of the church I Pastor, but came to the school of the Prophet, because the prophetic anointing in her life started to stale. She told me when she disconnected from me, the gift of vision went down as if she could not function properly in it. The moment she was reconnected to me, she started seeing how it happened the first time. A man walked in a service we were having and that man had a stroke two weeks prior coming to the church.

The moment he walked in the service, God healed him of the stroke. When he went to his doctor for further testing, the doctor told him that there was no signs of the stroke. His health was restored to him by God through the Prophet. God uses Prophets to restore the things you

The Prophet's Instructions

have lost and to give you direction concerning the now and the future. Jesus is our true example of what it means to walk in such office. His primary work was to restore what Adam lost through his disobedience (Genesis 3).

We need to appreciate and honor the prophets we are connected to. We support them in prayer, encouragement and financially. Most of us do not know how bless we are to have a Prophet in our midst.

The Prophet's Instructions

THE OFFICE OF THE PROPHET

The office of the Prophet was establish in the book of Genesis (Genesis 20:7). Now therefore, restore to the man's wife for he is a Prophet and he will pray for you and you shall live. Prophets do more than just prophesy. Abraham did not prophesy to anyone during his time, but he listened to God and followed Him.

We understand Prophets are called by God to declare what He is saying to the people. Later on in this chapter, I will show you the different type of Prophets we have in the bible.

The Prophet's Instructions

The office of the Prophet is sacred unto the Lord and not everybody is called to walk in such an office. There is prophetic gifting and those who walk in that office literally. I need to make this clear to you, flowing prophetically does not qualify one to be a Prophet.

A Prophet is someone who is called by God and not by your church nor by your affiliation. We understand how God chooses someone and allow their leaders to recognize their gifts. People cannot make you a Prophet. God was the one who called Moses as a Prophet to

The Prophet's Instructions

deliver His people out of bondage (Exodus 3:10). I have encountered people who call themselves Prophets because they want to be popular.

The office of the Prophet comes with warfare and it is a lonely place to be. The amount of warfare Prophets go through can be discouraging to the point where you want to give up. Can you imagine what someone who is called as a Prophet go through? Prophesying is great, but a lot of people cannot handle the pressure that comes with the office. Religious people are the ones who hate Prophets with a passion. How would you feel to know you are a true Prophet, while others are calling you false?

The things Prophets go through in their office will make you think twice before you accept your calling as a Prophet. I can recall how many times I was called a false Prophet. The interesting part is, the same people who were calling me a false Prophet would come to me to hear what God was saying concerning their lives when they needed a word. When Prophets do not allow themselves to be broken by God, the world will make you forsaken your office. I am talking from experience and not something I have heard. Here is what I mean by the statements I made previously concerning the office of the Prophets.

You must be a strong person mentally when it comes to you walking in the office of a Prophet. You have those who love your gift, but hate you because you carry the title of a Prophet. Prophets, be mindful of those who will not celebrate you publicly, but always want to hear what the Lord is saying for them through you. People must honor the Prophets the same way

47

they love their gift. Prophets must be celebrated and honored at all times.

Jeremiah was born a Prophet without any human validity (Jeremiah 1:4-5). Some are born Prophets before the foundation of the world. We see how Amos became a Prophet based on the necessity thereof. Then Amos answered and said to Amaziah: I was not a Prophet nor was I a son of a Prophet but I was a sheepbreeder and a tender of sycamore fruit. Then the Lord took me as I followed the flock and the Lord said to me, go prophesy to my people Israel (Amos 7:14-15). Amos let us know here he

The Prophet's Instructions

was not born a Prophet, but because God saw he was fit for the job, and He put the anointing on him for the task. I believe majority of Prophets today were not born as Prophet but became Prophets.

God is sovereign and knows where there is a need and who can be trusted for the need. It is okay if you were not born a Prophet, but as long as God selects you to be, you will go forth to do exactly His will. Amos was effective to fulfil his assignment just like any other Prophet. I will begin to tell you the different type of Prophets and where they fit. All

The Prophet's Instructions

Prophets are Prophets, but they were not the same.

Isaiah was an eagle eyed Prophet who saw the coming of Jesus years before He came. Jeremiah was a weeping Prophet for Israel and all he could do was cry for the people's sake. Daniel was a governmental Prophet who worked with King Nebuchadnezzar.

Ezekiel was a watchman for Israel meaning God used him through visions mostly. How do you know Prophet God called you to be? It is extremely important for Prophets to submit under the leadership of a

The Prophet's Instructions

Pastor. Prophets tend to be wild and do not want to sit under anyone because of their accuracy of their prophecy. Some Prophets believe that God wants them to be independent. When something is not covered, it gets spoiled.

Prophets who do not believe in submission will end up destroying themselves. I would advise the Pastors not to allow the Prophets who does not attend a local church off their pulpit. It is a dangerous thing when Prophets think they have arrived and do not want to sit under a Pastor. Being anointed means you are going to submit to someone who will hold you accountable. You can be an accurate Prophet but you lack submission.

When Prophets tell you that God is their Pastor, run away from them. Prophets, just because you are more accurate than your Pastor does not mean you cannot submit to him. I have this to say, where in the bible it does say Prophet have to be under an apostle? What if the person you are under does not have an unction to prophesy like you? Humility is the key to get deeper and higher in God. God resist the proud and give grace

The Prophet's Instructions

to the humble. Here is a danger
concerning the Prophets when it
comes to ranks. Aaron and Myriam
were Prophets like Moses but God
used Moses differently (Exodus 7:1-
2).

We are Prophets, but we do not
carry the same weight in the sight of
God. When we believe we are on the
same level spiritually with our
Apostles, Pastors and Bishop, now
we have lost it. Moses was a Prophet
like his siblings but he carried more
weight in the sight of God. When
leaders believe to be on the same
level as their Pastors and want to

The Prophet's Instructions

disrespect God's anointed ones, heaven will shut you down without you knowing it. We see how God took care of Aaron and Myriam when they put their mouth on the vessel of the Lord (Numbers 12:1-9).

I want you to understand something, never bad mouth your leader under any circumstances. God will not be pleased with you and you will pay the consequences for your actions. Well, they believed they were Prophets just like Moses until God strike them. Touch not my anointed and do my Prophets no harm (Psalm 105:15). This scripture

The Prophet's Instructions

is still vital for the church today concerning His Prophets. We cannot allow ourselves to talk bad about the person whom God has raised to take us to places we have never been before. young Prophets, remain humble under the man or the woman of God and see what God will do with you.

When you see people talking bad about your leader, just run as fast as you can. God will not let those who talk negatively about their leaders to go unpunished. When we Prophets, begin to disrespect our Pastors, God will intervene on their behalf without them knowing. Some of us are too common with God's Prophet to the point we lose respect for them. You cannot receive from someone you do not honor. Gehazi did not honor Elisha and we saw what happened when the Prophet did not take anything from Naaman (2 Kings 5:20).

You may not be in the sight of the Prophet, but he can see what you are up to. Gehazi thought Elisha could not see him, but the Prophet's spirit went with him when he received what Elisha did not want from Naaman. Elisha died with the

The Prophet's Instructions

mantle because the one who was serving him was greedy and did not listen to the voice of the Prophet. Elisha served Elijah and received the mantle through his willingness to serve the man of God. People who will serve you, but does not respect you, will not inherit your mantle.

Impartation only belongs to people who respect and honor you. The ones who are talking bad about but want your mantle will never receive it. We need to respect God's anointed or it will cost us even our lives. The Lord loves His Prophets, so should you. When God calls

The Prophet's Instructions

someone to be a Prophet, first, He separates you for Himself. Why does God separate us from people and family members?

He does it so He could train you for what He is about to use you for. A Prophet training is in the wilderness where God Himself begins to train you. In the wilderness, you have no one to depend on, but God. The wilderness shapes your character. It is in the wilderness we find our true identity in Christ. This place called the wilderness is the school where the Prophets go to in order to receive the training. In the

The Prophet's Instructions

wilderness you learn to walk by faith and not by sight. You will know someone is a true Prophet. It is when they pass all the tests in the wilderness.

I can hear you say, I do not think I am ready to go for training in the wilderness. Jesus was trained in the wilderness when the Holy Spirit led Him there (Matthew 4:1-11). The wilderness equips you to be victorious in warfare. After Jesus came out of the wilderness, He was ready to shake the world with the power of the Holy Spirit. In the wilderness, you learn how to fight

The Prophet's Instructions

with Satan day and night. The
wilderness produces an anointing that
heals the sick and to set people free.
Beloved, the wilderness can be hard,
but God will not anoint you without
the wilderness.

The wilderness gets dark at
night, but the Holy Spirit will be your
guidance. You cannot declare the
spirit of the Lord is upon me without
the wilderness. The anointing you
need to fight the battles is in the
wilderness.

Now, how does someone flow
as a Prophet? Remember all Prophet
do not flow the same way. The

The Prophet's Instructions

number reason that will help
someone to flow like water in the
prophetic is knowing the word.
Without the word of God, you will
not be able to flow prophetically.
Learn to develop an intimacy with
the Holy Spirit. Thirdly, you
environment can make you flow or
kills your flow. When you are
around the right environment, it
causes you to bubble up
prophetically. Prophets and prophetic
people must surround themselves
with other prophetic people.

You see when Mary visited
Elizabeth, John the Baptist was filled

The Prophet's Instructions

the Holy Spirit and he leaped because Jesus was next to him (Luke 1:41). One thing prophetic people do not understand is this, the right environment will thrust you into your destiny while the bad one will cause you to be stagnant. Why is your environment so important to you when it comes to flowing prophetically?

In our church, when I see people begin to leap in the prophetic, I encourage them to go forward. There are environments you get into that will cause your gifts to suffocate. What I have come to understand is

The Prophet's Instructions

this, most people who say they are midwives are really abortionists. Midwives help you to push and encourage you to keep on pushing until the baby comes out. While the abortionists are those who see the baby coming out and do whatever they can to kill the baby. Again, when you are around the people who are not jealous of your anointing, you will go far.

Prophets go through frustration during their time of training. At times, God will strip you naked from everything you have possessed. Meaning, He removes everything away from you that stands as a hindrance for Him, so that He can train you. Prophets go through the word test during their training. The word test is something Prophets go through to test their character and motives.

When a Prophet releases a word to you, that same word will test and challenge you. This book is a small token of my heart to you and I pray you enjoyed reading it. Many people have the gift of prophecy where they can hear what the Holy Spirit is saying for themselves or someone else. The gift of prophecy

The Prophet's Instructions

is not the office of the Prophet.
Earlier in this chapter, I talked about
being in the right environment for
your gift to grow. The gift of
prophecy is not the office of the
Prophet.

Being filled and baptize with
the Holy Spirit qualifies someone to
prophesy if they want to. Here is the
difference, you can pray to God and
ask Him for the gift of prophecy, but
you cannot ask Him to make you a
Prophet. Pursue love and desire
spiritual gifts but especially that you
may prophesy 1 (Corinthians 14:1).
There are gifts I did not have, but I

prayed and the Lord saw me fit for them and give them to me. Again, do not use the gift of prophesy to make others feel small. Arrogance will get you in trouble if you are not careful. When God is using you in the gift of prophecy it comes and goes.

At times we ask God for this gift, He doesn't give it to us, because our motives are wrong. The more the Holy Spirit is using you, the more humble you should be. I have seen people get healed when they come to my meetings, but that never change me nor made me think I am the best in town. Women who could not have children were able to get pregnant and give birth under my ministry. I have seen God cancel debt in my ministry several times and it never made me puffed up.

Prophets, please learn to respect Generals in the gospel. God uses men to help men, therefore be careful how you treat others. The office of the Prophet needs supervision. Samuel was a Prophet but the Lord raised him under the tutelage of the priest, Eli (1 Samuel 3). You cannot be all that God called you to be on your own. There is a necessity in the prophetic for mentors

The Prophet's Instructions

and spiritual fathers. There is more to
the office of the Prophet than just
prophesying. Even until today, I
remain connected to my mentors.
Miracles do not move me nor the
accuracy of the prophetic word I
release. What moves me is the Father
pleasing with what He has called me
do. I am just an instrument in the
hands of my Master.

Prophets and prophetic people,
never ever allow people to make you
prophesy in the flesh. Some will
offer you money to make like Balaam
to prophesy (1 Kings 18). The
Prophets of old used this word here,

The Prophet's Instructions

thus saith the Lord. If the Lord is not saying anything remain quiet please. Prophets hear me and hear me well. God did not call you to pimp His people. You have to understand when God calls individuals, He makes provision for them. Prophets you are not a psychic nor a fortune teller.

Prophets of God are always misunderstood by people who cannot see where God is taking them. Have you ever imagined, the people who should have supported you and those are the same ones to make you abort you assignment. Let me say this to your spirit, only a Prophet can raise a

The Prophet's Instructions

Prophet. When I found out I was a Prophet, I only allowed prophetic people to be in my circle. God sent a lot of Prophets to teach, encourage, love, push, believe and mentor me when I first started.

They were not afraid of my gift and the way God was using me. What amazed me was some of the people who told me where God was taking me were the same people who became jealous when God started using me. Be careful not to allow people to contaminate your gift through greed.

The Prophet's Instructions

In a couple of paragraphs, I will tell you how God speaks to me. He speaks to me in dreams, visions, trances and through my heart which is my spirit.

When I minister during preaching, the Holy Spirit speaks to me in my heart. I am a dreamer who dreams things that will take place in the near future. I see visions a lot while my eyes are open which is not night visions. We wonder at times why God is not speaking to us during the day. The response is, we are too busy with the things of life.

The Prophet's Instructions

My ears are always attentive to hear what God is saying concerning me or others. As a Prophet, when someone comes in my presence to hear what the Lord is saying concerning a matter, I do not need to get on my knees and start praying.

Prophets should develop ears and hearts to hear what God is saying in the now. I have challenged a lot of Prophets when it comes to the now word. Some will say they are not hearing anything. A doctor is a doctor no matter the time or the season you see them. They may not have a scrub

The Prophet's Instructions

but they are still doctors. My prayer
has always been for the Lord to use
me at all times. There are places I go
to, I have to shut myself down and
stop prophesying. When you are in
the room where the people
expectation is high, God will speaks
to you more.

What I do when there is a lot of
people, I bring the sons and the
daughters to flow as the company of
the Prophets. What makes you flow
better in the prophetic is when you
have people believing in you and
give you opportunities. Lack of
submission will kill your prophetic

The Prophet's Instructions

flow. When your leader corrects you and you remain offended, it will cause your prophetic ability to decrease. Be aware of unforgiveness because it causes your anointing to dry.

My prayer for you as you finished reading this book. May the Holy Spirit endow you with a fresh anointing that catapult you into a level you have never been to before. I declare you walk in the prophetic more than ever. May the Lord guide and open your mouth to speak the mysteries of heaven.

23253630R00041

Made in the USA
Columbia, SC
10 August 2018